Violence in **Society**

Nigel Smith

Wayland

Global Issues series
Crime and Punishment
Genetic Engineering
Racial Prejudice
Terrorism
United Nations: Peacekeeper?
Violence in Society

Editor: Merle Thompson
Series Editor: Cath Senker
Designer: Simon Borrough

First published in 1995 by Wayland (Publishers) Ltd, 61 Western Road, Hove,
East Sussex BN3 1JD, England

Acknowledgement
The author is grateful for the assistance of Mrs Pat Wales, Librarian at Hall
Mead School, Upminster.

British Library Cataloguing in Publication Data
Smith, Nigel
Violence in Society. – (Global Issues)
I. Title II. Series
660.65
ISBN 0 7502 1512 7

Typeset by Simon Borrough
Printed and bound by G. Canale C.S.p.A., Turin, Italy

Cover picture: A fight in a street in Germany leaves one of the
participants bleeding.

Title page picture: This girl has been pushed to the ground and her belongings
scattered by a thief attempting to snatch her handbag.

CONTENTS

AN INTRODUCTION TO VIOLENCE

When a person kills or injures another, an act of violence occurs. We live in a violent world. Every minute of the day, someone becomes a victim of violence. Many people have to cope with violence as a normal part of their everyday lives when war destroys their homes, schools, hospitals and crops. At any one time, there are as many as 30 million refugees throughout the world who have been forced from their homes by war. Even in countries free from war, acts of terrorism or violent crime can strike anyone without warning.

Violent robbery in the street (mugging) is increasing in many cities throughout the world. Often, both the victim and the robber are young.

In this book we shall look at some of the different kinds of violence around the world. Opinions differ about the causes of violence but, in every chapter, questions and issues will be raised to help you form your own opinions.

Violent crime

Even in countries with a high standard of living, people are increasingly worried about rising crime. Although most statistics show that violent crime makes up a fairly small proportion of all the crimes committed in any one country, violence causes substantially more harm to its victims than any other crime. Newspapers and television in Europe and America continually warn the public about rising violence. Many people are fascinated by violent crime whether it is real, or the fictional kind shown in books, films and television shows. Violent crime has become an important political issue.

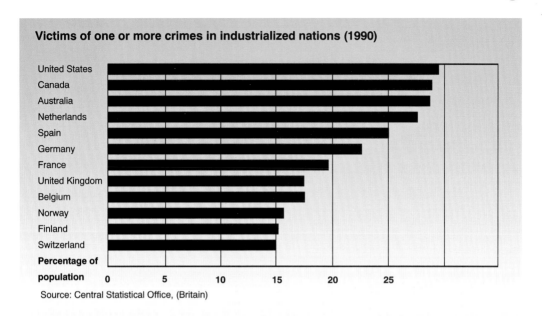

Victims of one or more crimes in industrialized nations (1990)

United States
Canada
Australia
Netherlands
Spain
Germany
France
United Kingdom
Belgium
Norway
Finland
Switzerland

Percentage of population 0   5   10   15   20   25

Source: Central Statistical Office, (Britain)

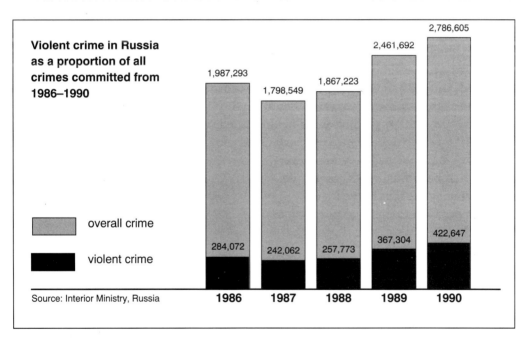

Violent crime in Russia as a proportion of all crimes committed from 1986–1990

overall crime

violent crime

	1986	1987	1988	1989	1990
overall crime	1,987,293	1,798,549	1,867,223	2,461,692	2,786,605
violent crime	284,072	242,062	257,773	367,304	422,647

Source: Interior Ministry, Russia

The causes of violent crime

Why should some individuals be more aggressive than others and commit acts of violence? Most people have their own ideas about what causes violent crime, but most would agree that there is no one simple cause. Some believe that people must take full responsibility for any bad things they do. If they have difficulties in their lives, they should exercise self-control and, if

they do not, and cause harm to others by their actions, then they should be punished. Others point out that society as a whole must bear part of the blame.

Sociologists, researching into the causes of crime, have indicated many different things which might cause people to become violent criminals. Some have suggested that unhappy experiences in childhood can cause some people to become disturbed. Often, this problem is made worse by overcrowding, poverty and bad housing. Other people have brought attention to the high importance given to material possessions, especially in the West, and suggest that many criminals who are poor or underprivileged may take, often by violent means, what they feel they cannot obtain in any other way. Some people can become desperate because of poverty. Much violent behaviour amongst young people, especially when linked to vandalism, has been found to be the result of boredom or a way of expressing anger, or frustration. Many youths in the inner cities see violence as a way of confirming their membership of a particular group or gang and, where guns are easily available (as in the USA), this behaviour is even more dangerous.

Mindless vandalism causes damage which can cost a great deal of money to clean up and repair and can cause people to feel threatened in their own neighbourhoods. Many young vandals blame boredom for their actions.

FACT FILE

The main causes of crime
According to a MORI opinion poll in January 1994 British people think the causes of crime are as follows:

drugs	72%
unemployment	71%
lack of parental discipline	69%
lenient sentences for offenders	51%
lack of discipline	44%
poverty	44%

Poverty and violence

People living in poor underdeveloped countries often face violence. Life in the *barrios*, the poor neighbourhoods of South American cities, or in the overcrowded slums of Calcutta in India, has always been brutal. Mahatma Gandhi (1869–1948), a political and spiritual leader in India said: '*Poverty is the worst kind of violence*'. It is a short step for the desperation of poverty-stricken people to turn into violence.

Rising unemployment and the lack of opportunities for young people are sometimes blamed for the increasing amount of crime in inner-city neighbourhoods. Some people, with a great deal of spare time and very little money, can easily turn to drugs and crime.

War

Arguments over territory have always led to violent conflict. In the nineteenth century, Europeans massacred millions of native Americans as they took over their homelands. Sometimes racial and religious intolerance causes bloody civil wars or conflict between nations. During the Second World War, Hitler tried to kill all the Jews in Germany and in occupied Europe. In the African country of Rwanda, the struggle for power between the Tutsi and Hutu tribes has resulted in the slaughter of thousands of families. Some states, like Bosnia, have split along ethnic lines.

Civil wars, such as the one which occurred in Rwanda in 1994, cause terrible suffering to people who are already desperately poor. Most of the victims of civil wars are civilians who cannot protect themselves against armed soldiers.

World-wide there have been more than a hundred major conflicts during the past forty years that have cost the lives of at least twenty million people.

Lack of political freedom

Sometimes, governments behave violently towards their own people and use police and the army to crush any opposition. Occasionally entire groups of people use violence in pursuit of justice and a better way of life. There have been many examples of this in the past, such as the French Revolution of 1789, and the Russian Revolution in 1917. During the 1980s, students protested in the township of Soweto against the South African Government. In a world where 800 million people still do not get enough to eat and others have no fundamental freedoms, it is not surprising that there is so much violence.

Is violence always wrong?

Most people would claim to be against violence but there are occasions when violence might be considered acceptable. Public opinion has frequently supported a country going to war. Today armies use very sophisticated, highly technical weapons, which sometimes kill more civilians than soldiers. However, many people believe that it is still justifiable to fight for a cause that they think is important. An example of this was the struggle against the Nazis and their allies during the Second World War. Only a small number of people are pacifists who are not prepared to use force under any circumstances.

Some people have always enjoyed watching violent sports just so long as they are not themselves in any danger. The Romans organized spectacular contests between gladiators who were slaves trained and then forced to fight each other to the death. In a single day in 50 AD, over 5,000 animals, including elephants, tigers and leopards, were killed for the entertainment of a huge crowd. In more recent times people have flocked to public executions or floggings. Even today, public executions in China still draw large crowds.

In the past, it was thought that cruel methods of public execution would deter people from crime. Here, in the year 1326, a British nobleman is executed for treason. Today, some countries, like Britain and France, have abolished the death penalty.

In the industrialized nations, young people can often spend many hours watching violent programmes on television. There is strong disagreement amongst some people over whether or not violence in entertainment can lead to greater violence in society.

In many countries throughout the world bloodsports, leading to the violent death of an animal, remain popular entertainments. In some ways these activities might remind us of Rome two thousand years ago.

Boxing and wrestling, which are both very violent activities, are part of the Olympic Games. In these cases, within the rules of the sport, violence is perfectly legal and acceptable.

Our approach to violence can therefore be selective. We may criticize violent behaviour but, in the case of a war we support, or a sport we enjoy, we may actually approve of violent behaviour. Many people enjoy watching violent films, videos and television programmes. Violence is a deeply ingrained and established part of the twentieth-century world.

‘ ’

• • •

Fascination with violence
Peter Marsh, in his book *Aggro*, published in 1978, wrote: '*Our [the British] current fascination with violence is almost unique. We protest an abhorrence of fights, injury and murder, yet we manufacture more images of violence in the name of news and entertainment, than of any facet of human behaviour. From reading the breakfast newspaper to switching off the late-night movie we become more and more convinced that our societies are reaching new peaks in the business of chaotic self-destruction. We are outraged and appalled. But we are also vicariously aroused. For when the effects are indirect, violence is fun.*'

How can we stop violence ?
Many people and organizations
are devoted to trying to reduce
and stop violence. The United
Nations was founded after the
Second World War to try to
maintain peace between
nations as well as to encourage
governments to respect human
rights. Many individuals have
tried in all kinds of ways to
further the cause of peace. The
Nobel Peace Prize is awarded
annually to someone who has
fought for peace in a non-
violent way. Dr Martin Luther
King was awarded the prize in
1964 because he had
courageously organized mass
peaceful protests against racial
discrimination in the USA.
Archbishop Desmond Tutu is
another Nobel Prize winner for
his tireless and always peaceful
campaign in the face of
violence to gain equal rights for
non-white South Africans.

In many communities there are
people working with young
men and women to provide
them with an education, skills
and job opportunities so that
they will not be tempted to
commit crime. Community-
based programmes like those
set up in some inner city areas

in the USA such as the South Bronx, New York and in
Ponce, Puerto Rico's second largest city, have been
very successful in helping young people to break free
from a life of crime. If people and governments
co-operate then perhaps some social problems such as
poverty, inequality and injustice can be removed so
that aggression and conflict may gradually decline.

In 1985, Archbishop Tutu
of South Africa was
awarded the Nobel Peace
Prize in recognition of his
courage in opposing the
repressive policy of
apartheid by peaceful non-
violent methods.

VIOLENT CRIME

Fear of violent crime is growing in many countries, but people cannot agree about the causes of violence or the best way to deal with the problem. In the high crime areas of inner cities, fear of violence can make people feel trapped and frightened to leave their homes.

Just how serious a problem is violent crime? It is not always easy to tell from official crime figures, as so many crimes are not reported to the police. But, for example, in Britain, the risk of being violently attacked is quite low – about once in every 250 years. There is a much greater chance of being killed in a road accident. Media reports of violent crime can sometimes give the impression that the problem is more serious than it really is.

FACT FILE

Public fears in the USA
Question: In your community, do you think that violent crime is more of a problem than it was ten years ago, less of a problem than it was ten years ago, or about the same?

Not sure	4%
Less	5%
About the same.	37%
More	54%

Source: National Victim Center, USA, 1991

Fear of being attacked or robbed can stop people, especially women and the elderly, from going out of doors, particularly after dark. Their fears may be unjustified, for sensational news and television reports can make people think the streets are more dangerous than they actually are.

Who are the victims and why?

The majority of victims of violent crime know the person who attacks them. The most common reason for murder is an argument in the family or between friends. Many attacks are said to be 'victim precipitated' – that means that the victim may have provoked the incident that led to his or her injury.

Who commit the majority of violent crimes?

Men commit the majority of violent crimes and most victims are male. In the USA, which has a higher crime rate than most other industrialized, democratic nations, assault is most often committed by a young, poor, male, from a minority group, on someone like himself. Over half of the murder victims in the USA since 1980 have been black Americans, with the majority under the age of thirty. These usually are people who live in the inner cities where there is high unemployment and a great deal of gang and drug-related crime.

The increasing use of guns

In the USA, there has been a large increase in violent crime linked to the use of guns during the

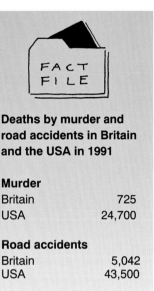

FACT FILE

Deaths by murder and road accidents in Britain and the USA in 1991

Murder

Britain	725
USA	24,700

Road accidents

Britain	5,042
USA	43,500

Total population

Britain	57,649,000
USA	248,709,873

Source: Central Statistical Office, Britain
National Center for Health Statistics and FBI, USA

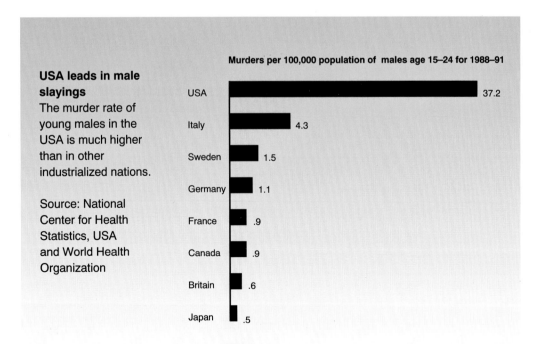

USA leads in male slayings
The murder rate of young males in the USA is much higher than in other industrialized nations.

Source: National Center for Health Statistics, USA and World Health Organization

Murders per 100,000 population of males age 15–24 for 1988–91

USA	37.2
Italy	4.3
Sweden	1.5
Germany	1.1
France	.9
Canada	.9
Britain	.6
Japan	.5

Homicide records set in 22 cities

The USA appears to be on track for a record number of homicides in 1993, shattering the brief lull of 1992.

A USA TODAY survey of police departments finds 22 major cities already have set homicide records in 1993.

'We're going to have another record this year, I know it' says St Louis police spokeswoman Christine Nelson.

There were 24,703 homicides in the USA in 1991 and 23,760 in 1992, an almost 4% decrease.

Nelson blames the 1993 rise on access to guns, which figure in most homicides.

'There are lots of guns in the hands of our youth,' she says.

USA Today, December 1993

past twenty years. Despite recent laws aimed at controlling gun sales, it is still easy for people, including convicted criminals, to purchase handguns. Most of the victims, as well as the criminals, are young men. In 1990, handguns killed twenty-two people in Britain, sixty-eight in Canada and eighty-seven in Japan while, in the USA, 10,567 people were killed by guns. It is estimated there are at least 211 million guns in the USA. That is enough guns to arm every adult and more than half the children. The US Justice Department estimates that, in some inner-city schools, more than one fifth of boys own guns and many of them carry them all the time.

The increased popularity of drugs such as crack cocaine appears to be one of the main causes for the increase in violent crime in inner-city areas.

In many parts of the world it is easy to buy guns from dealers like this one on the North West Frontier between Pakistan and Afghanistan. These guns could end up being used by criminals, drug smugglers or terrorists.

Should the sale of guns be controlled?
The real solution to violent crime is to shoot back.
'*If the person accosted by a criminal is likely to be armed, if the home owners are presumed to have guns, most criminals will think twice before mugging, raping or burglarizing … you can't defend yourself with a gun control law.*'

An anti-gun control view in *USA Today*, December 1993

We must stop glamorizing guns.
'*We need greater gun control measures and we need to re-examine our glamorization of guns and violence. It's tragic when our children feel the need to obtain guns and can carry them so easily.*'

A pro-gun control view in *USA Today*, December 1993

Knives

Although the use of guns is increasing amongst criminals in Europe, there are very strict controls on who can buy and keep them. Far more people carry knives but, with a knife in one's pocket, it is all too easy for an argument to turn into a deadly fight.

The impact of drugs

Violent attacks are often the result of alcohol or drug abuse and many robberies are also drug related. Crime linked to drugs is not a new problem but it has risen dramatically in recent years. The British police estimate that drug addicts and users are responsible for between a third and a half of all thefts. Drugs are blamed for half the violent crime in the USA, while Spain and Germany have particularly serious problems of drug-related crime. Perhaps it is significant that Japan, with a low rate of drug offences, also has a murder rate below that of Britain.

Drug taking is a very expensive habit and can be fatal. Some drug addicts commit violent acts, out of desperation, in order to pay for their habit.

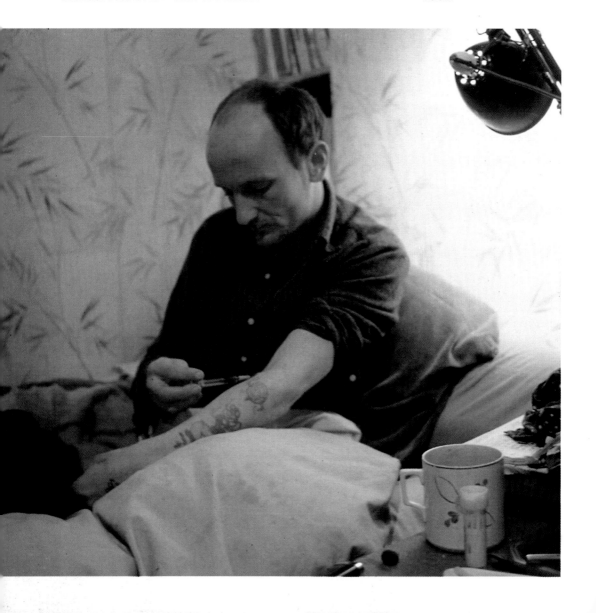

Drug-related violent crime

Police forces have become alarmed at the spread of drug-related violent crime, fuelled by easy access to firearms and the high profits from drug dealing.

'Several users who committed armed robberies in Oxford last summer pleaded crack addiction in mitigation. As the drug trade grows, fears for safety have widened. Drug-related crime is rising out of control. Police and politicians now accept that no one escapes the drug explosion as growing amounts of burglaries, muggings and theft are committed to buy narcotics. In West Yorkshire, [Britain] firearms offences have more than trebled over the last five years. Detective Chief Inspector Blakeley said: "It's like watching an epidemic with the drugs itself." '

Source: The *Independent,* London, March 1994

Should drugs be legalized?

It is argued that if some hard drugs were made legal there would be less violent crime.

'The Head of Interpol called for the decriminalization of drug use saying resources would be better targeted at drug dealers and education programmes. Those calling for controlled legislation of harder drugs say it would reduce associated crime, ensure greater health and safety of users, and destroy some lucrative black markets. They cite prohibition in the USA in the 1920s, which saw an explosion in violent crime directly related to the black market in alcohol – a parallel with today's crack gangs.'

Source: The *Independent,* London, March 1994

Not only is crack cocaine a dangerous drug but drug dealers use violence against one another to keep control of their profitable business.

Violent crime in Russia
Including assault, armed robbery, murder and rape

Source: Interior Ministry, Russia

Addicts need a regular supply of money to pay for their drugs, and, if necessary, will resort to violence to get it. Inner-city violence and shootings have increased as drug dealers fight each other to control the drug trade. Those who take part in it can earn vast sums of money. A 1987 survey in Washington DC, in the USA, found that there were 11,000 regular drug traders in the city who had a combined income of around $30 million a year. In spite of attempts to stamp out the international drug trade, well-organized, violent, criminal gangs continue to supply hard drugs to Europe and the USA. In Russia since the collapse of the Communist government in 1991, drug-related crime has rocketed and violent crimes, including murders, doubled in the ten years up to 1992.

Singapore's answer to violence
Muggings are virtually unknown here because brandishing a knife in public (even without using it) earns three to five years [in prison] and six strokes of the cane. Armed robbery is rare because discharging a firearm in the course of a crime (whether anyone is hit or not) is punishable by hanging. Possession of a firearm gets a mandatory twenty years.

There are millions of people in Britain and America who yearn for some Singaporean steel in the way thugs and yobbos are dealt with.

Source: *Daily Mail*, London, March 1994

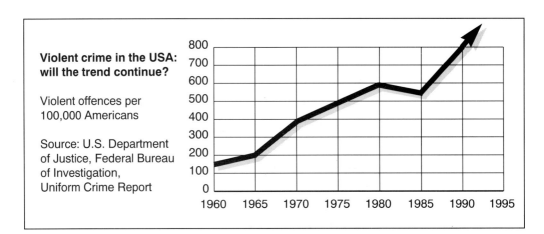

Violent crime in the USA: will the trend continue?

Violent offences per 100,000 Americans

Source: U.S. Department of Justice, Federal Bureau of Investigation, Uniform Crime Report

Is punishment the answer to violent crime?
Some say that tougher punishment is the answer to violent crime. To the public, who are concerned by growing violence, it seems reasonable to blame the criminals for their actions. Severe punishments may deter others from carrying weapons and committing crime. Some states in the USA still have the death penalty as the ultimate punishment for murder, but is the principle of an 'eye for an eye' the right approach? The number of people in prison in the USA is, proportionately, the highest in the world, yet the murder rate is still far higher than that in Europe. Are long prison sentences therefore not the answer to violent crime? Putting people in prison will stop them committing crimes while they are there but, by the time they leave, many of them may have become even more hardened criminals. The answer to violent crime is not a simple one.

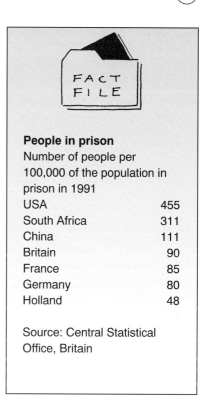

FACT FILE

People in prison
Number of people per
100,000 of the population in
prison in 1991

USA	455
South Africa	311
China	111
Britain	90
France	85
Germany	80
Holland	48

Source: Central Statistical
Office, Britain

As crime has risen, so more people have been sent to prison. But the frequent use of punishments such as imprisonment does not seem to have halted the rise in violent crime.

RACIAL VIOLENCE

It is very hard for most people to understand what it must be like to live in constant fear of being attacked because of their race or colour. But, for millions of people, in many countries, racial or ethnic violence is a very real threat in their daily lives. Sometimes, as in the case of the Kurds in Turkey and Iraq, the governments are responsible for the violence. The worst example of ethnic violence occurred in Germany during the 1930s and 1940s, when Adolf Hitler and his Nazi Party were responsible for the murder of more than six million Jews.

This home in London (right) was painted with hostile slogans just before an Asian family was due to move in. Pigs' feet were also nailed to the doors.

What is racism?
You may have laughed at a joke that poked fun at someone because of their race. You may also have heard people insulting others because of the colour of their skin. Black and Asian people in Europe, for example, have to put up with name-calling and worse every day. Racial prejudice, that is the belief that one race of people is superior to and better than another race, can easily lead to violence.

This Jewish cemetery has been vandalized by racists who have daubed Nazi swastikas on the gravestones. Some people today still admire the racist policies of Hitler and threaten Jewish people with violence.

FACT FILE

Racial attacks in Britain

1988	4,682
1990	7,095
1991	7,780

Most attacks are not reported and the Anti-Racist Alliance estimates the actual figure as around 70,000 attacks each year.

Racism in Britain

On average, over twenty racial attacks take place every day in Britain. People from racial minorities are sixty times more likely than white people to be targets of an attack. Asian women and children usually suffer the most and often can live in constant fear. People are afraid to open their doors or let their children go out to play or even walk to school on their own. In just one part of London, Greenwich, more than 1,000 racist incidents were recorded in 1993, including many racial assaults on women living on council estates.

It is estimated that only about one in ten racial attacks is actually reported. People are sometimes too frightened to go to the police or give evidence in court. The government and the police have been accused of ignoring the rapid growth in racial violence, which has increased considerably since the early 1980s.

MEDIA WATCH

Racial attacks, including murder, have reached unprecedented levels in Britain. Last year eight people were killed as a result of racist attacks, according to anti-racist monitoring groups, who say the problem is being widely ignored. They say, '*Racist violence has never been so hidden and unacknowledged as it is in this country*' and '*There is a holier than thou attitude in this country which has allowed them [the government] to sweep racist attacks under the carpet*'.

Source: *Guardian*, London, February 1993

The rise of Fascist political groups

Who are the people responsible for this violence? Many of the attacks on black people in Europe are carried out by gangs of white teenagers. These attacks may start with racist taunts – sometimes a repetition of the kind of comments teenagers have heard their parents make. But the influence of extreme right-wing or Fascist political groups in many European countries is much more alarming. Fascists, who admire Adolf Hitler and believe that the white race is superior to others, believe that violence is an acceptable way to deal with those they hate. These organizations encourage gangs of youths to attack 'foreigners'. Jean-Marie Le Pen, the extreme right-wing leader of the French National Front, has won a great deal of support by blaming black immigrants for unemployment and other social problems. Politicians like Le Pen exist in many countries. In Australia, Fascists have attacked Vietnamese and Chinese refugees. Italian skinheads have assaulted North Africans. Although neo-Nazi groups in Britain have always been poorly supported, they have been able to stir up racial violence in some inner-city areas.

The actions of British right-wing extremists (right) can cause considerable fear and tension, especially when they march through areas where many black and Asian people live.

German skinheads (left) give the Nazi salute to show their support for racist ideas. Older people who remember the Holocaust, when millions of Jewish people were murdered by the Nazis, are horrified by these demonstrations of hatred.

A few convinced Fascists can cause a great deal of tension and fear. Many of the young whites who take part in racial attacks or support Fascist policies are unemployed or have low incomes and perhaps very little in their own lives that they can take pride in. Racists exploit the stress caused by high levels of unemployment, housing shortages and poor public services, and blame other races for these problems. As unemployment rose in the early 1990s people looked for someone to blame. In Germany the newspaper, *Der Spiegel*, summed up this attitude: *'The Germans have been gripped by fear, fear of strangers, fear for their jobs.'*

Fascist groups in Germany

In Germany, the government estimates that there are 40,000 right-wing extremists, of whom 4,000 are violent skinheads. There have been thousands of attacks on people who the extremists consider to be 'foreigners'. In November 1992 a firebomb attack on the home of a family of Turkish origin in the German town of Mölln caused the deaths of two little girls and their grandmother. A chilling phone call to the fire department was made by someone who said: 'Fire in Ratzeburger Street! Heil Hitler!' Ten-year-old Yeliz Arslan, one of those killed, was born in Germany where her parents had lived for twenty-three years. A similar attack six months later killed two women and three girls in their home in Söllingen. Most Germans were appalled and thousands marched through the streets in silent protest against this violence. The head of the German government, Chancellor Kohl, described the killings as a 'disgrace for Germany'. But violent attacks against minority groups have continued.

German Fascists marching through the streets of Halle, Germany to shouts of 'Germany for the Germans'.

The Ku Klux Klan

Racial tension has always been a serious problem in the USA. It has often led to violence. Black Americans are descendants of the slaves forcibly taken from Africa. For two hundred years, millions of Africans suffered brutality as slaves. But even when they finally achieved freedom at the end of the Civil War (1861–65) many whites were not prepared to treat them as equals. Racial discrimination and violence against black people continued. The Ku Klux Klan has, for more than one hundred years, used violence as part of its campaign against the rights of black Americans. The Klan, a white supremacist organization, was set up after the Civil War to make sure that black people did not achieve the same rights as white Americans.

A protest rally held by opponents of racism after the arson attacks against Turkish people in Söllingen, Germany, in 1993.

Klan members dress in robes with hoods that hide their faces. They set fire to large wooden crosses that can be seen for many miles. Their slogan is 'white power!' Throughout the 1920s and 1930s, when the USA was suffering from the Great Depression, the Klan had 5 million members and many of these were politicians and police officers. A dreadful part of the campaign to 'keep the black in his place' was the 3,500 lynchings of black men and women that took place between 1882 and 1964. Those responsible were hardly ever brought to justice.

When unemployment began to rise in the 1990s, more white people began to support the Klan, blaming black people for the lack of jobs. Although the Klan is far smaller than it was sixty years ago, racial attacks began to increase. Nowadays, its victims include other racial groups such as Asians, Mexicans and Jews. In 1991, the Klan claimed to have doubled its membership while 101 cross burnings were reported compared to 50 the previous year.

In the USA, the Ku Klux Klan wear long gowns and carry crosses and Confederate flags from the American Civil War at their meetings. They claim that the white race is superior to any other.

'Poor whites, resenting what they see as jobs, housing and welfare being handed out to minorities at their expense, are looking for scapegoats. The Klan reproduces a code of racism and hate and is able to infect society when conditions are right, and conditions are right now … I believe race relations in the United States are going to continue to worsen and the influence of hate groups is going to increase.'

An anti-Klan view expressed in *The Sunday Times,*

Civil rights in the USA

Dr Martin Luther King led black Americans during the 1950s and 1960s in their fight to end discrimination. He preached the ideal of non-violent protest as a form of resistance to racial violence. Demonstrations, marches and other peaceful protests, including the Great March on Washington, helped bring new civil rights laws to make discrimination illegal. But laws do not necessarily change people's minds. It was Dr King who warned: 'We must learn to live together as brothers or perish together as fools.' In 1968 Dr King fell victim to violence when he was assassinated by a white gunman.

During the 1950s and 1960s, peaceful civil rights demonstrators in the USA were often roughly treated by white police officers.

YOUNG PEOPLE AND VIOLENCE

On some large housing estates in Britain, people often feel threatened by gangs of young people who can sometimes be responsible for vandalism and violent crime.

According to a 1993 Gallup opinion survey, nearly half of Britain's teenagers know another young person who has attacked someone or broken into a car. The truth is that young people have always rebelled against their elders and been responsible for a great deal of crime. Sometimes older people speak of the past as if it had been 'a golden age' when young people behaved themselves and accepted authority. The same complaints were probably made by their elders about them when they were young.

Has crime increased amongst young people ?
In the nineteenth century, English apprentices, as young as fourteen years of age, caused many problems. Gangs of young people roamed many industrial towns looking for amusement and often caused trouble.

People thought that work was the best answer to this problem and John Locke, a well-known political writer, recommended in 1797 that children of the poor should begin some form of work at the age of three. Victorian London had many gangs of children called 'street arabs' or 'ruffians'. These children called themselves hooligans and caused terror with their battle cry, 'Boot him!'

A minority of young people enjoy vandalizing and destroying property. It is difficult for others to understand why this should be so but, in many cases, the quality of life of these young people is very poor.

They may have taken their name from Patrick Hooligan who was a 'chucker-out' at a pub, and who is said to have died in prison after killing a policeman. More recently, young British gangs have adopted all kinds of names including 'Teddy Boys', 'Mods', 'Rockers' and 'Skinheads'. Even if they have not the slightest intention of committing violence, the sight of a large number of young people, wearing the uniform of their particular group, can be frightening.

MEDIA WATCH

Young hooligans – little changes
In Continental cities, or in the USA, they have very little scruple about calling out troops and shooting down organized disturbances of the peace … But if we do not adopt Continental methods of dealing with street lawlessness … if we do not wish our police to be formidable as an armed force, we must not grudge an increase in street violence.

Source: *The Times,* London, 17 August 1988

Football violence

Britain invented football and, sometime later, football hooliganism. During the past thirty years it has been exported to many other European countries. Some football 'fans' have become increasingly violent and have even caused a number of deaths. The behaviour of British football supporters in 1985 led to the deaths of thirty-eight others, mainly Italians, at the Huyssel Stadium in Brussels. The tragedy led to English football clubs being banned for a time from playing European matches. Even though the violence comes from only a small group, it has been difficult to prevent. At the 1990 World Cup in Italy, English fans rampaged through the streets of Cagliari. In 1993, serious fighting in Oslo left the city looking, according to one newspaper reporter, 'like a war zone' after riot police were called to deal with English fans.

They just want to fight
Drunken English soccer yobs rampaged through Amsterdam.
'The boozed-up mob hurled bottles and glasses in a running fight with police. At least 125 louts were arrested and six policemen injured as the battle raged. As last night's mob ran riot, one senior police officer said: "The English, always the English. All they want to do is fight. It is true our own fans are not angels. But these English fans are just animals – we have never seen such behaviour on our streets." '

Source: *Daily Mirror,* London, October 1993

There have been times when a football stadium has resembled a battlefield. This scene at the Huyssel Stadium in Belgium was described as the 'Battle of Brussels'. More than 3,000 police struggled to keep order in a riot that left thirty-eight people dead.

Why do young people commit violent crime?

Why do young people, particularly males, want to behave in this way? Unemployment may be one cause of crime, but most football hooligans are not unemployed. More likely their violence, often made worse by excessive drinking, results from aggressive feelings towards opposing teams and their fans.

These young Germans seem to be just as interested in causing a disturbance as they are in watching the football game.

In most industrialized nations there are now large numbers of young people without jobs living on low social security benefits. Unemployment, poverty and family breakdown mean that many young people do not feel part of the mainstream of the society in which they are living. They feel like outsiders. They are powerless to improve their

Thousands of young people survive living rough on the streets of major cities all over the world. They are victims of a society that seems to offer them few opportunities. It is not surprising if some of them end up as criminals.

own standard of living and often see no hope for the future. A few young people may commit crimes simply to obtain things that they want. But they may also commit acts of violence out of frustration and anger. Their victims are nearly always people who are weaker and less powerful than they are.

Who is in prison in Britain?
Over 80% of the young offender population is white, working class and male. Only one in every forty young offenders is female ... Only one in five girls and one in six boys is in prison for violent offences.

Source: The Prison Reform Trust, July 1993

Why do they do it?
We may not care that young men are killing themselves. We may suppose that young men have only themselves to blame for being by far the most likely victims of violent assault. They are after all, the ones who commit it, too. But does any sane society really wish to fill its streets with unemployed, ill-educated, dissatisfied young men? The consequences, in terms of crime and social disorder are far too obvious to ignore.

Source: *Daily Telegraph,* London, March 1994

Once the only way for a man to prove his manliness was in war. The gangs of today which destroy property and attack people seemingly without reason are obeying this inherited urge.

Source: *Daily Mirror,* London, March 1972

With little to occupy their time, unemployed youths often turn to aimless vandalism and violence.

Can violent protest be justified?

'*Riots*', said Dr Martin Luther King, '*are the voice of the unheard*'. Many young people throughout the world take part in political demonstrations. Young people are often quick to oppose injustice and are willing to challenge their government. Because they have few family or other responsibilities, they may be prepared to risk danger in violent confrontation with police and soldiers. In 1956, young people played a major part in the Hungarian uprising against Soviet rule that was brutally crushed by the Russian army. In 1968, young students in Paris fought pitched battles with the riot police as they protested against the policies of the French government. Then, in 1994, French high school students took part in demonstrations over unemployment and the government decision to cut the youth minimum wage.

For more than thirty years, young black people demonstrated in South African townships against the system of apartheid. Under apartheid, black people had no say at all in the government of their country. They were often violently attacked by the white police and soldiers and many of them were killed. Apartheid was finally brought to an end in April 1994, when the first elections, at which blacks as well as whites could vote, were held. Nelson Mandela, who had been held prisoner as a terrorist for twenty-six years, was elected as the first black President of South Africa.

The former Portuguese colony of East Timor was seized by the Indonesian Government in 1975. Since then, there have been many protests, especially by students, against oppression and the lack of human rights in their country.

Violence against young people

As a result of young people's political idealism,
sometimes the state itself uses violence against
young people. During the Vietnam War, thousands
of young Americans protested against their country's
involvement in the war in mass demonstrations.
Many young men refused to be conscripted into the
army. In 1970, four young students at Kent State
University were shot dead by soldiers during a protest
against the war. A father of one them appealed:
*'Have we come to such a state in this country that a
young girl has to be shot because she disagrees deeply
with the actions of her government?'*

There have been many other instances when people,
often young people, who have rebelled against their
government have, in the end, been proved justified.

Many schoolchildren and
university students
demonstrated against the
South African system of
apartheid as here, in
1986, in the city of
Johannesburg. Often
these demonstrations
were violently broken up
by the police and a
number of people died in
police custody. Apartheid
has now been replaced by
a democratic system in
which all South Africans,
black and white, are able
to vote.

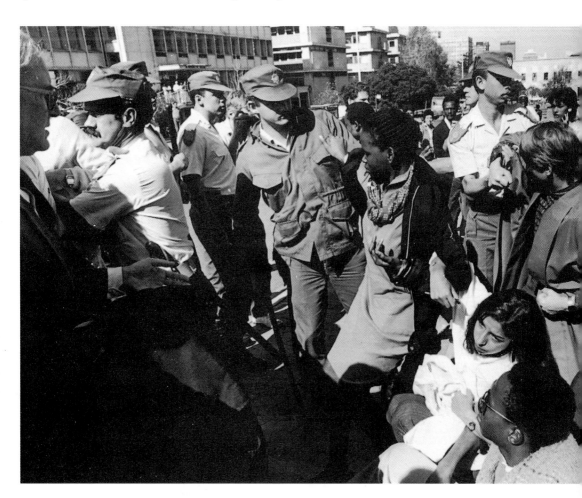

CHILDREN AND VIOLENCE

The Rights of Children

The United Nations Convention on the Rights of the Child says that: *'Children have a right to life and the best possible chance to develop fully. Children have the right to be protected from all forms of violence. They must be kept safe from harm. They must be given proper care by those looking after them.'* Unfortunately, many victims of violence are children who suffer at the hands of those who are supposed to protect them, including their parents or the state. Neglect and poverty, as well as the violent behaviour of adults around them, can also lead children to commit acts of violence themselves.

Children at war

All children are affected by wars, particularly by the disruption that is caused by a long-running civil war. Children in these circumstances grow up in an atmosphere of hatred and violence. Children living in the Israeli-occupied West Bank and the Gaza Strip were caught up in the *intifada*, an uprising that started in 1987 against the Israeli occupation of their land. They took part in violent demonstrations and threw stones at Israeli troops. Many were injured, and some killed, by Israeli soldiers. In Northern Ireland, during the 1970s, young Catholic children joined the rioters who attacked British soldiers.

Following the break-up of the former Communist country of Yugoslavia into separate states, a vicious civil war broke out. Children have been forced to grow up in an atmosphere of fear, hatred and violence.

Children are not only victims of civil strife but sometimes play a part in the fighting. This boy is throwing rocks at heavily armed Israeli soldiers in the Gaza Strip. Many children have been killed in similar incidents.

Life and death in Sarajevo, Bosnia, 1992
'Some days the shooting is worse than others. I've had many friends who were hurt and one of my friends, Nina, was killed. We knew each other since we were babies and she was good friend…we used to play in the park together, the same park where she died. I don't understand this war. I don't know why it started. It kills and it kills and it makes no sense.'

Zlata Filopovic, thirteen years old, writing about life under siege by Serbian forces.

FACT FILE

The land where children are killed
Violence has been a way of life in Israel and the occupied territories. Up to 1993, five Israeli children were killed during the *intifada* by terrorists. But many more Palestinian children were killed by Israeli soldiers.

Palestinian children killed by security forces in the occupied territories

	Under age 13	Age 13–16	Total
1987–88	8	40	48
1988–89	29	50	79
1989–90	5	21	26
1990–91	14	20	24
1991–92	4	13	17
1992–93	13	26	39
	73	170	233

Source: B'tselem (an Israeli human rights group), 1993

This boy was fighting in the civil war in Lebanon during the 1980s. Child soldiers often grow up believing that violence is a normal part of everyday life.

MEDIA WATCH

Death in Colombia
It's six o'clock in the morning. An eight-year-old boy called Gustavo Marroquin leaves his house to join his father, who is in the milking shed. Two hundred metres from home he freezes. Out of the landscape emerge camouflaged figures, armed soldiers of the Colombian army's 18th Infantry Battalion. They shout to the child, but he is frightened and turns to run home to his mother. The soldiers fire. Again and again. Their bullets lift the child and fling him to the ground. His mother hears the shooting, runs out. Sees. Screams. The soldiers will not let her go to her little boy. He dies where he fell. That is how eye-witnesses saw it. The army's story is that they saw not a terrified eight-year-old child, but a dangerous guerrilla.

Source: *Amnesty International Report*, 1994

Some children have even been enlisted as fighters in recent wars in Afghanistan, Angola, Central America, Iran and Mozambique. The United Nations Human Rights Centre has estimated that world wide there are 200,000 child soldiers. The *Mujahadeen* (holy warriors), a Muslim guerrilla army that fought the Russian-backed government in Afghanistan during the 1980s, conscripted boys as young as nine. Often children are keen to fight because they think it will earn them the respect of adults. Child soldiers and other children caught up in riots and demonstrations, have been captured and imprisoned. During the 1980s, the South African Government detained nearly 10,000 black children without trial.

The street children

On the streets of cities in many developing countries millions of children struggle to survive. Poverty-stricken families living in overcrowded slums and shanty towns cannot always look after their children. Many are forced on to the streets to scratch a living. India has the greatest number of street children. In each of the cities of New Delhi, Bombay and Calcutta there are around 10,000 street children. They struggle to survive by begging, collecting rags and shining shoes. Inevitably, many of them turn to crime. The worsening poverty of African countries has led to similar problems. In 1989, Nairobi, the capital of Kenya, had about 16,000 street children. Four years later this number had risen to 25,000.

These children live in poverty and squalor on the streets of Calcutta, India and have never known the security of a proper home. Children like this can easily become victims of violence.

There is a very uncertain future for these children in Bogota, Colombia. Many such young lives have ended violently at the hands of vigilante death squads or even the police.

'The big-time killers are still free'
Over the last two years Tania Marias Salles Moreira, a public prosecutor, has stalked dozens of alleged killers of Brazilian kids...her targets – hit men hired by drug dealers and merchants' associations – are often untouchable in the courts as well as on the streets: they routinely terrorize witnesses, bribe judges and thwart investigations. Many of the killers are cops themselves. But Tania persists, *'The Brazilian people need to be reminded that there is a basic right that comes before any other, the right to live. If we don't secure this right, nothing else matters.'*

Source: *Newsweek*, New York, 25 May 1992

Throughout South America, large numbers of abused and neglected children live on the streets. Many of them live a nightmare existence, frequently coming into conflict with the police and in danger of being abused or murdered.

Many children are forced to steal simply in order to survive. Some are used as couriers by drug dealers. Gathering together in gangs, they are seen as a nuisance, frightening customers and tourists away from shopping areas. Many adults are frightened of the children and want to see them removed. They have no wish to concern themselves with why the children have no proper homes and have ended up on the streets.

The Brazilian police put the average number of child murders during 1988–91 at more than 1,500 a year. In 1991, about 1,000 died. International child welfare agencies say that, apart from countries caught up in war, Brazil's children are dying violently in numbers unmatched anywhere else. The head of the United Nations Children's Emergency Fund (UNICEF) in Brazil has said:

'Maybe there are countries with a higher rate of murders of children in proportion to the total population. However, given the absolute numbers of murders, Brazil is really a phenomenon of its own.'

What is particularly shocking is that many of the killings have apparently been carried out by police officers or vigilantes hired by local businesses. Death squads have targeted the youngsters they blame for crime in the knowledge that few people care what happens to the children so long as they simply disappear.

In another South American country, Colombia, some concerned people have set up a remarkable charity, 'Los Niños de los Andes' (Children of the Andes), to provide education and help for many of these children who have nobody else to care for them.

Charity workers manage to help some street children by providing them with food and shelter. But many more resources are needed before the problems that put them on the streets in the first place can be solved.

Child abuse

Violence against children takes place all over the world. According to the FBI, US children under eighteen were 244 per cent more likely to be killed by guns in 1993 than in 1986. The estimated number of child abuse victims increased by 40 per cent between 1985 and 1991. In Britain, too, violence can be a daily experience for increasing numbers of children. Sometimes it is at the hands of their parents who are supposed to be protecting them. In 1994, 47,000 children were on the Child Protection Register because of fears that they might be hurt by their parents. The National Society for the Prevention of Cruelty to Children warned that British children were being killed at the rate of three every week by their parents.

Sometimes violence in a child's life is caused by other children and takes the form of bullying or even robbery. Teenagers stop other youngsters to steal watches, trainers or mountain bikes. Bullying can be a serious problem that can cause great distress but is often not taken seriously enough by adults. As one teenager put it: '*If adults are bad-mouthed in public it's called slander and if adults are hit or kicked around its assault. But if it happens to us it's called bullying and adults don't take it seriously enough.*'

Surge in child slayings

Children under 18

1,400	_____
1,200	_____
1,000	_____
800	_____
600	_____
400	_____
200	_____
0	_____

Source: FBI

This boy (right) plays with a toy gun even though his wound was caused by a sniper's bullet in Sarajevo, Bosnia in 1993.

Violent games in a school playground which sometimes lead to bullying.

Between 1986 and 1992, shootings of children in the USA have risen 143% compared with 30% for adults.

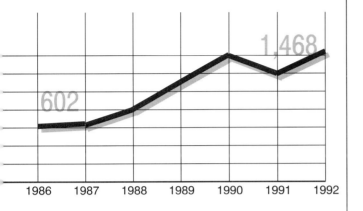

What is bullying?
It's being picked on, victimized. If it upsets you then it's bullying. Here are some examples:

Emotional bullying: Picking on someone because they are different, perhaps overweight, small, have a disability or don't wear trendy clothes.

Racism: Picking on someone from a different racial background or making fun of their culture.

Assault: Punching, hitting, tripping up or physical violence of any kind.

Taxing: Threatening someone to get their money, trainers or other gear.

Sexual bullying: If someone pressurizes you for sex or to go further than you feel happy about it's bullying. Don't put up with it.

Source: *Young Express*, London, May 1993

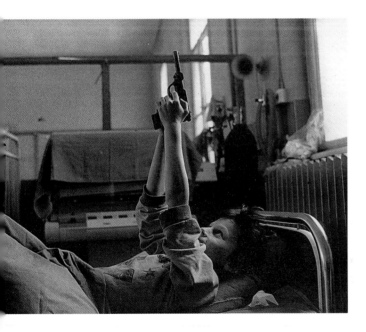

What happens to children who are victims of violence? Children who suffer, or witness, brutality at an early age are much more likely to be brutal and violent to others when they have grown up. Today's violence means that the next generation of children is also likely to suffer at the hands of those who have themselves been victims of violence.

WOMEN: VICTIMS OF VIOLENCE

In many countries, women do not have the same educational opportunities as men. Often, they have had little say in the making of laws or in the decisions of government. Just over 10 per cent of the members of the parliaments throughout the world are women. In 1993, only six countries had a women heading their government. But, throughout history, women have been forced to bear a great deal of suffering caused by the political decisions of men that have led, for example, to war.

In times of civil war and famine, women often suffer most as they struggle to feed and look after their children. This Somalian woman has fortunately reached a source of aid, but many such families died during the civil war in the early 1990s. .

These desperately unhappy women are mourning the deaths of their husbands killed during a terrorist attack in Sri Lanka in 1989.

FACT FILE

Women's health
Women tend on average to live longer than men. However, in some Asian and North African countries, the discrimination against women – through neglect of their health or nutrition – means that they have a shorter life expectancy. In Bangladesh, Bhutan, the Maldives and Nepal, women actually have lower life expectancies than men. Indeed, comparing the populations who should be alive, based on global mortality patterns, it seems that 100 million Asian women are missing.

Source:
United Nations, 1993

Even in peacetime, women from every social class, ethnic group and in every country of the world, are treated violently. Because they are physically weaker than men, they may be more easily attacked, raped, threatened or insulted. In some countries the problem can made be worse by the fact that they have a low status in society and are not protected by law in the same way as men.

The status of women

In some countries, boys are more valued than girls. Tradition, religion and the law stop many women from having productive or well-paid work. So, where there is great poverty, boys are far more likely to get more of their fair share of food and health care. In South Asia, men and boys eat first and the women and girls share whatever is left. Consequently women are far more likely to be malnourished. In some Amazon villages, more than twice as many women suffer from malnutrition as men.

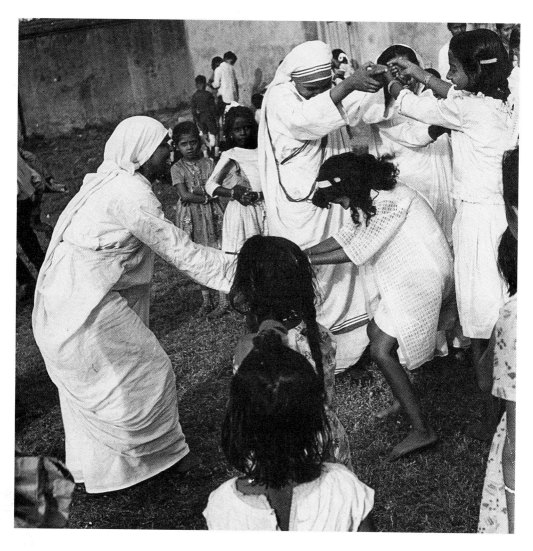

These nuns belong to a religious order founded in India by Mother Teresa to help the poor and destitute. Much of the nuns' work involves caring for children who have been abandoned by their parents.

Unfairness towards women is particularly marked in parts of India where many baby girls are killed at birth by their parents. This female infanticide is usually tolerated by local people and, even though it is officially against the law, the authorities find it very difficult to stop. Local people think the practice sad but unavoidable. The tradition that a father has to provide a dowry, a sum of money, for his daughter before she can marry, is the cause of these infant deaths. For people who are very poor, this may be impossible. It is common for people who are better-off to pay to find out the sex of their unborn baby. Then, if it is female, it can be aborted. In the mid-1980s in a single Bombay clinic about 16,000 female foetuses were aborted each year. Of course it is easy for well-off people in Western countries to criticize these terrible practices without thinking about the poverty that gives rise to them.

Attacks in the home

A considerable proportion of the violent crime in relatively well-off European countries and the USA is directed against women. Women are not safe even in their own homes. In Britain about 80 per cent of all women who are murdered are killed by someone in their family or a close friend. By far the biggest single category of killer is the husband or ex-husband. About a quarter of all violent attacks reported to the police are on women attacked by their partner at home. Yet crimes of domestic violence are not always seen as being as serious as attacks on strangers or murders that take place during robberies. Every year the police in London receive about 100,000 calls from women reporting attacks by their partners. Only about 10,000 of these attacks are recorded by the police as being crimes. Yet each of those attacks could potentially turn from bad bruising or broken bones into a case of murder. It is clear that, as one expert says: '*If we are to deal effectively with violence in our society, we must deal effectively with domestic violence.*'

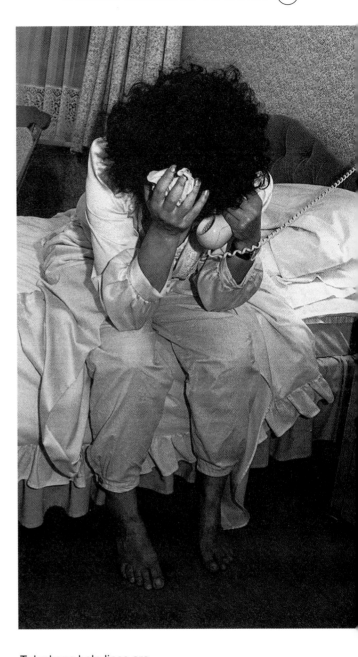

Telephone help-lines are available in some countries to provide advice and support to women who have been violently abused.

What makes a woman kill her husband? And can she expect a fair trial?

Driven to destruction

EVERY YEAR, about 15 women in the UK kill their husbands. Although many of them have faced severe domestic violence in their marriages, this fact is rarely taken into consideration in the courts.

The only complete defence against a charge of murder is a claim of self-defence. But three conditions must be fulfilled: the defendant must show that she did what a reasonable person might have done in the same situation; the threat to which she reacted must be seen as proportionate to the violence she committed; and the danger must be imminent.

British courts have generally been reluctant to accept that these conditions might not apply to a woman who retaliates against domestic violence.

Source: *Guardian*, London, February 1991

Victims of violence at home

Bangladesh	Half of the 170 reported murders of women, from 1983–85, were within the family.
USA	Between 3 million and 4 million women are battered each year but only 1% of the incidents are reported to the police.
India	Five women are burned in dowry-related deaths each day.
Austria	In more than half of divorce cases, domestic violence was given as a cause of marriage failure.
Trinidad	The number of men charged with rape rose by 134% from 1970–80

Source: United Nations, 1993

Violence begins at home

A Spanish riddle: What do mules and women have in common?
A good beating makes them both better.

'This has been with us for as long as we can remember: men have attacked, beaten or raped their wives throughout history. It may be illegal now but we still have to change the attitude the community has grown up with.'

A West Yorkshire police officer in *Woman's Journal*, London, June 1991

'The law may have changed but the attitude lingers on. Society still doesn't understand that it is as much of a crime to assault your wife at home as it is to attack a stranger in the street. The result is broken bones and dead bodies.'

A domestic violence counsellor in *Woman's Journal*, London, June 1991

Why are some women badly treated?

For centuries, the law in most countries treated women as if they were the property of their husbands. Although in many countries this is no longer the case, the idea that women should obey their husbands and that they are there to serve them persists. When a women refuses to accept this idea, she may be attacked. Boys who have witnessed their father attacking their mother may grow up seeing this kind of behaviour as a normal part of family life. Many of the men who attack women have grown up in violent circumstances themselves and been corrupted by violence.

Women who are frequently attacked live in a state of permanent fear and may have nobody they can turn to for help. Often they have children to consider, very little money of their own and nowhere they can go to which is safe from their husbands. Many women are too ashamed to admit that they have been abused.

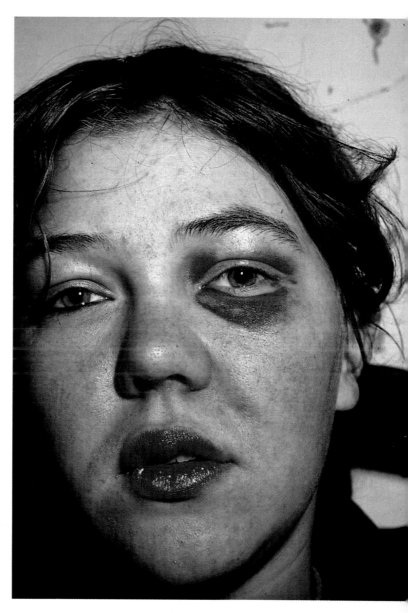

Many women who are attacked by their partners suffer injuries like the one shown in this picture.

What should be done to tackle this serious problem of violence? In Canada the government has taken the problem very seriously. Many women's refuges have been set up across the country where women, who have been attacked by their partners, can live in safety.

Police officers have been specially trained to deal with domestic violence and have consequently taken more offenders to court. The cycle of violence that seems to exist in some families has been tackled through education. The Canadian approach is not only based on the fact that it is right to stop violence but that to do so will save money. If fewer women are attacked, it will save the cost of police time and hospital care. Showing that violence against women in the home will not be tolerated and helping women to escape from it, is one of the most important crime prevention measures that society can undertake.

Women's refuges, like this house in London, provide somewhere safe for women to go, with their children, if they are threatened by a violent partner at home.

Rape

In most countries, sexual assault on women is the single most under-reported crime. In the USA, rape is increasing four times faster than other crimes. Even though the crime figures show that men suffer most violent attacks, women still fear for their safety if they walk alone at night. Some women have organized demonstrations to 'reclaim the night'. They say that their freedom to go out at night is being taken away from them by men.

Governments as well as individuals need to do more to help prevent violence against women. Some progress has been made. In 1991, the European Community adopted a 'Code of Practice for the Protection of the Dignity of Women and Men', intended to stop sexual harassment at work. Since 1986, the United Nations has urged its members to take more action to protect women from violence in their homes. Other countries, including Australia, Argentina as well as those in Europe, have begun to follow the Canadian example. What do you think needs to be done in your country to reduce violence against women?

Various measures can make women feel safer at night, including better street lighting and reliable public transport. Some women take classes in self-defence, or in a sport like Judo, so that they can feel more self-confident when walking alone, especially after dark.

VIOLENCE AS ENTERTAINMENT

The average child in the USA has, according to the American Psychological Association, watched 8,000 murders on television and 100,000 acts of violence by the time he or she is eleven years old. A 1993 study of British television revealed that in a single week more than 400 killings, 119 woundings and 27 sex attacks were shown on the four television networks and satellite channels. Most of the murders were shown on two of the satellite channels. Why do so many of us enjoy a lot of nasty and unpleasant violence presented as entertainment? But much more importantly, does the enjoyment of violence in entertainment affect people's behaviour?

FACT FILE

Violence on television in the USA

	Children's TV	Adult prime-time TV
Violent acts per hour	32	4
Violent characters	56%	34%
Characters who are victims of violence	74%	34%
Characters who are killers or get killed	3.3%	5.7%
Characters who are violent or victims	79%	47%

Source: Survey 1991–92, Professor George Gerbner, Annenberg School of Communications, University of Pennsylvania

A survey by the Broadcasting Standards Council in 1993, revealed that the amount of violence on television was the main concern of viewers, with 66 per cent saying that they felt that there was too much. Concern over 'too much violence' is partly

based on the belief that violence on television, and in movies, actually encourages people to commit violent acts. But is that really true? There is a great debate in the developed countries over a possible link between violence in entertainment and a rise in violent crime. Mary Whitehouse, a long-time campaigner against violence on British television said in 1964: *'If you constantly portray violence as normal you will help to create a violent society. People learn from watching others.'*

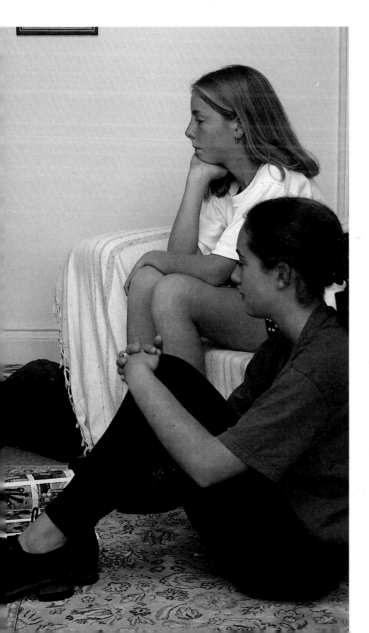

MEDIA WATCH

We must protect young minds
It seems quite possible that exposure to images of brutality could turn an already disturbed child towards violence. Certain films may have the effect of making violence acceptable to some children. The problem is not knowing what children should be protected from. Images of violence abound even in cartoons. Is it dangerous to show the Roadrunner dropping lumps of concrete on his hapless victim? What about Sylvester's efforts to eat Tweedy Pie and Tom's bloody adventures with Jerry? Is violence alright provided the good guy kills the bad guy?

Source: *Independent,* London, November 1993

Young people can spend much of their free time watching television. Many popular programmes show violence of some kind or another. Some people have become concerned that watching violent programmes on screen may encourage people to behave more aggressively in real life.

'I'm quite sure these horror and violent films will give your child bad nightmares, but horror films are designed to horrify, they do not themselves make the children horrific people. Poor parenting is a more likely cause of crime.'

Source: Dr Guy Cumberbatch, a psychologist at Aston University, in *The Times*, London, November 1993

Experts have admitted that they seriously underestimated the effects of screen violence on children. In an amazing U-turn twenty-six top specialists conceded they have been 'naive'. Professor Andrew Sims said: *'Watching specific acts of violence has resulted in mimicry by children and adolescents of behaviour they would otherwise, literally, have found unimaginable.'*

Source: *Daily Mail,* London, April 1994

Distressing images of the fighting in Vietnam eventually turned public opinion against the involvement of US troops in the war.

Reporting violence

Could it be said that television only shows the violence that occurs throughout the world and is not itself the cause of violent crime? Is it a case of wanting to shoot the messenger? Michael Grade, the head of a British television company, compared the blaming of television for violence with the beheading of bearers of bad news in ancient Greece. *'Television'*, he said, *'is blamed for encouraging violence because politicians haven't the foggiest idea how to stop crime.'*

A great deal of the violence we see on television comes from real life. Films of the dead and seriously injured are frequently shown in television news and documentaries. Recent wars including the Gulf War, and the fighting in Bosnia and Somalia have had extensive coverage. Pictures of people killed and wounded in the civil war in Rwanda caused a world-wide reaction of horror. By seeing for ourselves, even though we are in the safety of our homes, the violence being inflicted on other people, we may want to try to do something to stop it or to help the victims. During the 1960s and 1970s, the violent images of the Vietnam War shocked many Americans into demanding an end to the fighting.

A Vietnamese peasant during the Vietnam War faces interrogation at gun point by American soldiers. Pictures like this, when shown on television, bring the horror and misery of war into everyone's living room.

Computer games

In recent years, computer games have become very popular. Can some of these games affect young people's behaviour? One particular game that became popular with children as young as ten years of age involved running people over. Children and old people were the victims, and the players of the game saw a great deal of 'blood and guts' under the car when the people were killed. A British psychologist has warned, *'The real worry is aggression. If you play a video game, every time you shoot or kill somebody you get rewarded. The games are becoming closer to reality and this is worrying.'*

Computer games are very popular with young people. However, many of these games place the players in an extremely brutal fantasy world.

Many films that are meant only for adults are sometimes watched by children at home.

Censorship

Should governments ban violent computer games or films? This is a difficult question because some people think they should be allowed to make up their own minds about what they watch. It is interesting, however, that Scandinavian countries, with a great deal of freedom, especially on matters of sex, have strict controls on violence.

Some very violent games are only supposed to be played by adults but they can fall into the hands of children. Parents do not always prevent their children from watching films which are meant for older people.

In spite of extensive research it cannot be said with absolute certainty that films and television are or are not a major cause of crime and violence. Would it be right to ban these films for everybody just because a small number of people might commit violent acts as a result of watching them?

Other forms of violent entertainment

Long before film or television was invented there were violent popular entertainments. Some of them, such as bear-baiting, cock-fighting and bare-knuckle boxing, have been outlawed in Europe and North America,

This stag has been killed in France, in the name of sport. Increasingly people ask whether animals should be hunted merely for the entertainment of humans.

although they still take place in secret. Dog fights take place in Bangkok, Brazil, Venezuela, Malta and Moscow. One Moscow lawyer justifies dog fights: *'They are bred as fighters, so what is the problem? It's a sport just like any other.'*

Bullfighting is considered a great Spanish tradition. It is surrounded by ritual and the skill of bullfighters is greatly admired so that they can become extremely famous and highly paid. But the end result of every bullfight is the violent death of the bull. If the bull fails to co-operate in the build-up to its slaughter then it is punished by being stabbed with two 'banderillas' – long, steel-tipped, harpoons. The doomed bull is wounded several times before finally being killed. This 'entertainment' is enormously popular. In reply to criticism, the devotees of bullfights might point to the popularity of fox-hunting in England, hare-coursing in Ireland, stag-hunting in France and to other sports that end in the violent death of an animal.

Opponents of bloodsports cannot understand how people can enjoy violence that inflicts suffering on an animal. Do you think those who take part are as cruel and bloodthirsty as their critics say they are?

Since 1945, more than 300 boxers world-wide have been killed and the British Medical Association says the sport should be banned. Its supporters argue that boxers choose to fight and that it is less dangerous than some other sports. But it may seem strange that spectators enjoy watching two men exchanging blows, each trying to score a knock-out blow on the other. Perhaps the popularity of boxing and bloodsports is proof that violence is acceptable, at least to some people, just so long as it is not committed by criminals!

Hope for the future
In spite of all the violence that you have read about in this book, you should not forget that there are many individuals and organizations working to reduce violence.

Boxing is a very controversial sport. If we are against violence, should boxing be banned?

The great hope for the future must lie with greater co-operation between people. If we want a peaceful world then we should not allow differences in race or religion to divide us. We all need to work together if we are to have safe and happy lives. However, so long as there is poverty and injustice, violence is likely to remain a problem.

GLOSSARY

anarchist Somebody who is against all laws and does not believe in any form of government.

apartheid The system imposed by the white government of South Africa in 1948 to keep white, black, coloured (mixed race) and Indian people separate, because of its belief that white people were superior.

Asians (common meaning in Europe) People whose family origins are in the Indian subcontinent.

black people A term originally applied to people whose skin is black, but now often used as a term for all non-white people.

democracy A form of government in which people elect their own rulers.

discrimination unfair treatment of a particular group of people because of their racial or religious background.

dowry A gift of money or goods that, in some societies, must be given by a bride's family to her husband on marriage.

ethnic group A distinct racial group or any cultural group that sees itself as separate from others.

Fascist A person who broadly agrees with the extreme right-wing views of Adolf Hitler, especially his racial hatred of Jews and non-white people.

FBI The Federal Bureau of Investigation, which is the most important US law enforcement agency.

genocide An attempt to kill everyone belonging to a particular racial, ethnic or religious group.

guerrilla A member of a rebel army fighting the government of his or her own country.

immigrants People, who for political, religious or economic reasons, move from their own country to live in another.

infanticide The killing of babies or very young children.

intimidate To threaten, bully or frighten someone.

life expectancy The number of years that people are, on average, expected to live.

looting Breaking into shops or homes during a war or a riot and stealing goods.

lynching A hanging carried out by a group of people without a legal trial.

Nazi A supporter of Adolf Hitler's National Socialist Party during the 1930s and 1940s.

NSPCC The National Society for the Prevention of Cruelty to Children, which is the main British charity concerned with the welfare of children.

nuclear weapons Powerful weapons that explode by using energy released from splitting atoms. A single bomb can kill millions of people.

political asylum The right to live in a country other than one's own which can be claimed by people who are persecuted in their own country on account of their race, religion or political beliefs.

prejudice Negative feelings about a group of people, that are not based on knowledge or facts.

rebellion An outbreak of violence against a government.

refugee A person who is forced to leave his or her country because of war, famine, disease or fear of violent treatment.

riot Violent behaviour by a crowd which can cause injury to other people and damage to property.

scapegoat A person who is blamed for the actions of somebody else.

sexual harassment The pestering or threatening of someone (usually a woman) in a sexual way.

state A country with its own government.

terrorist A person who uses extreme violence to try to force other people, usually governments, to do what they want.

United Nations An international organization set up in 1945 to help countries to work together to maintain peace and promote human rights.

BOOKS TO READ

Aitkens, Maggie *Should We Have Gun Control* (Lerner, Minneapolis, 1991)

Alibhai, Yasmin and Brown, Colin *Racism* (Wayland, 1991)

Donellan, Craig (Ed.) *Law and Order* (Independence, Cambridge, 1993)

Guernsey, JoAnn Bren *Should We Have Capital Punishment?* (Lerner, Minneapolis, 1991)

Harris, Neil *Drugs and Crime* (Franklin Watts, 1994)

Read, David *Crime and Punishment* (Wayland, 1991)

Rench, Janice E. *Family Violence* (Lerner, Minneapolis, 1991)

Sanders, Pete *Feeling Violent* (Franklin Watts, 1994)

Steele, Phillip *Riots* (Heinemann, 1993)

Picture Acknowledgements
APM Studios *title page*, 4, 12, 51, 52/3, 56, 57; David Hoffman 16, 17, 19, 20, 21, 28, 32, 42, 47, 49; Camera Press *cover, contents page* and 6, 7, 8, 10, 11, 14, 15, 22, 24, 25, 29, 30, 31, 33, 34, 36, 40, 41, 44, 46, 50, 54, 55, 58, 59; Mary Evans 9; Impact Photos 23 (© Danny White), 37 (© A Cordesse), 43 (© J. F. Joly), 45 (© Rune Enaken); Topham 26, 27, 35, 38, 39.

INDEX